Shapes

I See Circles

By Czeena Devera

2 Here is a small circle.

Here is a big circle.

4

Here is a rough circle.

Here is a smooth circle.

6

Here is a full circle.

Here is an empty circle.

Here is a hard circle.

Here is a soft circle.

Here is a moving circle.

Here is a still circle.

Here is a light circle.

Here is a heavy circle.

Word List

small	full	still
circle	empty	light
big	hard	heavy
rough	soft	
smooth	moving	

Here is a small circle.
Here is a big circle.
Here is a rough circle.
Here is a smooth circle.
Here is a full circle.
Here is an empty circle.
Here is a hard circle.
Here is a soft circle.
Here is a moving circle.
Here is a still circle.
Here is a light circle.
Here is a heavy circle.

CHERRY BLOSSOM PRESS

Published in the United States of America by Cherry Lake Publishing Group
Ann Arbor, Michigan
www.cherrylakepublishing.com

Photo Credits: © IamDOT/Shutterstock.com, front cover, 1; © Pixel-Shot/Shutterstock.com, 2, 3;
© aerogondo2/Shutterstock.com, 4, back cover; © Mega Pixel/Shutterstock.com, 5; © Tatyana
Abramovich/Shutterstock.com, 6; © dreii/Shutterstock.com, 7; © Bilevich Olga/Shutterstock.com, 8;
© Olhastock/Shutterstock.com, 9, 14; © Air Images/Shutterstock.com, 10; © StanislauV/
Shutterstock.com, 11; © lara-sh/Shutterstock.com, 12; © G-Stock Studio/Shutterstock.com, 13

Cherry Blossom Press is an imprint of Cherry Lake Publishing Group.

Library of Congress Cataloging-in-Publication Data

Names: Devera, Czeena, author.
Title: I see circles / Czeena Devera.
Description: Ann Arbor, Michigan : Cherry Lake Publishing, 2021. | Series: Shapes | Audience:
Grades K-1 | Summary: "Spot circles and identify opposites in this book. Beginning readers will gain
confidence with the Whole Language approach to literacy, a combination of sight words and repetition.
Bold, colorful photographs correlate directly to the text to help guide readers as they engage with the
book"— Provided by publisher.
Identifiers: LCCN 2020030244 (print) | LCCN 2020030245 (ebook) | ISBN 9781534179844 (paperback) |
ISBN 9781534180857 (pdf) | ISBN 9781534182561 (ebook)
Subjects: LCSH: Circle—Juvenile literature.
Classification: LCC QA484 .D48 2021 (print) | LCC QA484 (ebook) | DDC 516/.154—dc23
LC record available at https://lccn.loc.gov/2020030244
LC ebook record available at https://lccn.loc.gov/2020030245

Cherry Lake Publishing Group would like to acknowledge the work of the Partnership for 21st Century
Learning, a Network of Battelle for Kids. Please visit *http://www.battelleforkids.org/networks/p21* for
more information.

Printed in the United States of America
Corporate Graphics